Praise for *At the River I Stand*

What a gift Dan Day's words are to every human soul who will someday face the end of their life (i.e., all of us). His is a faith painted for us in conversation laced with candor, honesty, questions, objections, and doubt, along with comfort, assurance, and groundedness. With his writing he sets us all on a path of connecting with God about life and death in ways that are deeply real and life-giving no matter the number of our days.

—*Dorisanne Cooper*
Pastor, Watts Street Baptist Church
Durham, North Carolina

In his collection of prayer, poetry, and ponderings, Reverend Day shares with us all an intensely personal and honest conversation with God about faith, death, and dying. As a physician and a teacher, I found in his words lessons on the importance of listening for memories and meaning amidst the "business" of diagnosis and treatment of disease. As a Christian, I appreciate the brave space he creates in his daily talks with God for the full range of emotions, from doubt and fear to humor and gratitude.

—*Mitchell T. Heflin, MD, MHS*
Durham, North Carolina

I heard the words with trepidation in 2017, "You have a terminal disease." I immediately began reading everything I could find about dying. So far, I have continued health. How I wish I could have read Dan Day's record of his walk with God each day as he faces death with stage 4 cancer. He is a word master with honest, challenging, poetic, testimony with profound pathos. His paragraph on Easter is worth the price of the book with his insight that we are experiencing in death and resurrection what Jesus Christ experienced! I could not put it down until it was finished.

—*Larry L. McSwain*
Retired Baptist educator and author of
Open and Closed Doors: Memoir of a Survivor of the SBC Unholy War

Dan Day has been a faithful guide to people and churches for decades upon decades. As he treads the verge of Jordan himself now, his prayers remain an honest and pastoral comfort for us all who will also one day have to cross the River.

—*Rev. Ryon Price*
Broadway Baptist Church
Fort Worth, Texas

Dan Day explores in a poignantly personal way the intersection of long years of Christian formation, thought, and ministry with the experience of what he calls "my Lazarus life." His metaphors are both real and revelatory as they voice paradoxes of life and death, truth and trust, honesty and hope. His prayers are simultaneously patient, persistent, and penetrating.

—*Paul A. Richardson, DMA, FHS*
Professor Emeritus of Music
Samford University

At the River I Stand is a collection of profound prayers on death and dying. I found myself unable to stop reading Dan Day's incomparably crafted book, except when I was surprised by sighs, smiles, tears, and laughter. As a confessional journal of faith, hope, and love by one who is in the valley of the shadow of death, *At the River I Stand* may well become a classic.

—*Dr. Daniel Vestal*
Distinguished Professor of Baptist Leadership
Director of the Eula Mae and John Baugh Center for Baptist Leadership
Mercer University

Should you find yourself in a season of life when reading the prayers of others will be the closest you can get to actually praying, then this book is for you. It takes courage to pray regardless of the unexpected circumstances life can bring, and in a phase of life when pain and suffering could easily have isolated him from God and from others, Dan has pulled back the veil to invite us into his honest conversations with God.

—*Rev. Louisa Ward*
Dean for Spiritual Life and Campus Minister
Campbell University

Oh, the humanity! This is one of the great gifts of Dan Day's new book: It is based in real human experience, not theories or theologies. It is about real life and real death and the line between the two. For anyone who has ever sat in a doctor's office or hospital bed and heard bad news, Dan offers a word of hope from the depths of his own journey. These are not trite platitudes; these are words of life from someone who has walked through the valley of the shadow of death.

—*Mark Wingfield*
Editor, Baptist News Global

At the River I Stand

Smyth & Helwys Publishing, Inc.
6316 Peake Road
Macon, Georgia 31210-3960
1-800-747-3016
©2024 by J. Daniel Day
All rights reserved.

Cover and illustrations by Megan Grace Day
megandaycreations@gmail.com

Library of Congress Cataloging-in-Publication Data

Names: Day, J. Daniel, author.
Title: At the river I stand : conversations with God about dying and living
/ by J. Daniel Day.
Description: Macon, GA : Smyth & Helwys Publishing, 2024. | Includes
bibliographical references.
Identifiers: LCCN 2024008332 | ISBN 9781641734967 (paperback)
Subjects: LCSH: Life--Religious aspects--Christianity. | Christian life. |
Death--Religious aspects--Christianity. | Meaning
(Philosophy)--Religious aspects Christianity.
Classification: LCC BT696 .D38 2024 | DDC 248.4--dc23/eng/20240408
LC record available at https://lccn.loc.gov/2024008332

Disclaimer of Liability: With respect to statements of opinion or fact available in this work of nonfiction, Smyth & Helwys Publishing Inc. nor any of its employees, makes any warranty, express or implied, or assumes any legal liability or responsibility for the accuracy or completeness of any information disclosed, or represents that its use would not infringe privately-owned rights.

At the River I Stand

Conversations with God about Dying & Living

J. Daniel Day

Also by *J. Daniel Day*

If Jesus Isn't the Answer . . . He Sure Asks the Right Questions

Seeking the Face of God: Evangelical Worship Reconceived

Finding the Gospel: A Pastor's Disappointment and Discovery

Lively Hope: A Taste of God's Tomorrow

To Mom and Dad

Mildred Elizabeth Day
1916–1996

and

Emory Nelson Day
1910–2006

Contents

Preface   1

The Door   3

I. Arriving at the River   5

II. Waiting at the River   37

III. Just Beyond the River   121

A Word to the Reader   141

Resources   143

Conversations Alphabetized by Title   145

When the darkness appears and the night draws near,
  And the day is past and gone,
At the river I stand, guide my feet, hold my hand;
Take my hand, precious Lord, lead me home.
—Thomas Andrew Dorsey
"Precious Lord, Take My Hand" (1932)

Preface

These conversations were written over the course of a few months, but their origin reaches across my lifetime. As will soon be evident to you, this life was sculpted by a churchgoing family, Christian Scriptures, gospel songs and Sunday hymns, and fifty years of service as a pastor of churches in Oklahoma, Texas, Louisiana, Missouri, and North Carolina. Along the way a PhD in theology got thrown into the mix. In brief, for good or ill, church-stuff and God-talk have been my home for eight decades.

Even so, when I first thought about writing this book, the title that came to mind was *Preacher on the Ropes*. That spoke the raw truth of my condition, and therefore I should forewarn any reader that if you have had your fill of stories of preachers coming undone, this is probably not for you. Other readers, however, may be helped by knowing that some valleys are so dark that even clergypersons, the ones paid to be officially full of light, stumble and moan in that darkness. But I also hope you will hear me talking with Someone in this darkness. That's why the subtitle says these conversations are about living as well as about dying.

Except for the first conversation, which introduces the story behind all the others, I have made little attempt to organize them in any sequential order. I have occasionally dropped in a line or passage of Scripture that has felt like God's response to my words. You are free to roam, to read whatever or wherever you wish, because there is no plot to these pages. They are meant to be dipped into, argued or agreed with, puzzled or pleased by, and laid aside until next time. I release them with only one hope: that they may prompt your own reflections and holy conversations.

Who knows? By the time you read these words, my death may be a matter of fact. After all, part of the theme of these conversations is the inevitability of that event, the sureness of my dying. If my family has already had my homegoing service, I regret that you and I never met. But reckon on this: as you read my words, what remains mystery for you is now my marvel and delight.

Though I cannot shout assurances across the chasm that separates us (or is it only a thin curtain?), my hope is that the conversations on these pages might deposit into your soul one pilgrim's bludgeoned but enduring affirmation: "Be not afraid. Kindness rests upon the face of The Mystery holding us all."

The Door

Death is like a door, the wise one said
    a door through which we walk into a new life
But whether full of health or deathly ill
    I was not eager to approach that door
Yet, curiosity persisting, I sought nearby windows only to
    discover the slow breath and tears of many had frosted each
    or were they frosted by God
    a sneaky way of saying No Peeking
Long hours of countless days and sleepless nights
    I've spent, abrasives in hand, scrubbing this way and that at
    Those windows, hoping to steal a glimpse
    but stubborn they have stayed, opaque, forbidding
Once I mightily tried to pry one open only to learn
    these windows yield no more to crowbars than to snooping eyes
Even my hard-baked bricks hurled in rage fell in futility
So back to the dreaded door I limp and here I linger
    reluctantly nodding yes to wisdom's word
Death is the only vantage given
    to learn what lies beyond
    to see what miracle world awaits
But once we enter and behold it clear
the world we knew—once loved as home—is gone

Arriving at the River

*Why should certainties surprise us so,
like the day they say: "It's time to go"?*

Twenty-four Months

O Lord, my God, this first day of March 2023 impresses me as a good day to begin a record of our conversations about dying. It's not as though they are profound or novel. In fact, they seem rather unexceptional to me, but if it weren't for you and for these minutes talking with you, the past few months would have been desolate indeed. This morning it feels right to begin writing down some of these conversations in case someone else may someday find themselves down here by the river and want a companion.

To begin with, we both know I've never been much for a "daily quiet time," at least the kind my mentors taught and urged upon me. The least accurate label anyone could put on me would be "prayer warrior," but I cannot pout about that loss since I don't even like that term. I do regret that my soul is unquestionably a size or so small because of my slipshod prayer habits.

It's just that it's always felt more authentic to talk with you when my talking and my listening came from my "want to" rather than my "have to." Since I have taken this easier path all my life, it feels a bit awkward at this late date to alter a lifetime pattern of "want to." So here I am, wanting to talk with you—and keep a record of it—about the topic that's been front and center for me since September 2021: death.

That, as you know, was the month when the doctors told me I had stage 4 prostate cancer and that men with the same profile as mine lived on average about twenty-four months. I hadn't been keeping count of the frequency of our conversations, but I'm pretty sure I set a new record that month and it hasn't returned to "normal" since then. No doubt that's because life itself has not really been "normal" since then.

When dying is no longer what other people do but is what is about to happen to you, "normal" gets redefined. Death ceases to be a theological category, a discussion topic. Death becomes a threatening, ever nearer predator circling above you, an indifferent assassin eyeing you from every dark corner. It's not "normal" to feel stalked like that, and even though my bully has been chased away for the moment, I am an altered person.

In retrospect, I question my wisdom in pushing my doctor to put a number on my probable days. He was doubly careful to say any number was an imprecise average and not a certainty.

Nonetheless, I knew I had an average life expectancy of twenty-four months. I subsequently read one physician's advice when asked if dying patients ought to be told their status. He said yes, they ought to be told "the train is coming, but don't leave them standing on the platform too long."** I guess that was the good doctor's way of balancing truth and love. I know I was certainly in need of both as I stood on that

lonely platform facing the grimness of my daily-diminishing twenty-four months. Then, four anguish-filled months later, sitting in a prostate cancer specialist's office, I swallowed tears of stupefied gratitude when he told me there were meds that could greatly extend that number. I was incredulous, skeptically rejoicing that this was too good to be true. Simply swallowing some pills every day and getting an injection every six months could forestall the inevitable? Really? Thirty minutes later, my wife, Mary Carol, drove me to IHOP for a late breakfast, and after parking the car she thoughtfully went on inside, leaving me to sit there alone for several minutes to process what I had just been told.

That's when the dam broke, didn't it, Lord? I cried as I never, ever remember doing. Wails of joy. Tears too big to flick away. Sighs of relief. Gulps of wonderful life-renewing air! Bone-deep thanks said to you—and to hosts of unknown medical researchers. My days weren't so numbered, after all! Maybe I was going to live! I tell you, Lord, never have pancakes, scrambled eggs, and sausage tasted as good as they did that morning—and the young man serving them to Mary Carol and me probably never received such a generous tip. (It is amazing how much ridiculous generosity can overtake a fellow when he's been blown away by good news!)

In the next weeks, as my body began tiptoeing back to itself in positive response to the new meds, the prospect of a very different tomorrow crept over me. I slowly awakened to the new landscape of my life. I'd just spent hard weeks trying to reconcile myself to the fact of dying without giving way to resignation. (For some reason that emotional stance seemed most important to me.) But now, with the benefit of some high-powered drugs doing their magic, my terrain had shifted once again.

Day by day it dawned on me: this is my Lazarus-life, the life that has been handed back to me even though I had thought it ended.* "Yes, Dan, you are still standing on the platform, waiting for the train just as every other mortal is, even if they pretend otherwise. But you misread the schedule; your train hasn't yet arrived, so you are now a veteran—you're familiar with this territory. Now you know the train *is* coming for you—sometime." Dying has now firmly been chiseled in large letters on my involuntary to-do list.

To recall a line from a gospel song and thereby change the imagery abruptly and significantly, I often now feel as though I'm standing on the muddy shores of death's wide river, humming, "At the river I stand; guide my feet, hold my hand."

Some might think this sounds morbid. I'm sure I would have thought so only months ago. But I don't find it morbid anymore. I am just being as honest as I know how to be with myself and with you. I am trying to keep my Lazarus-life in healthy perspective, and ironically this keeps me keen to the marvel of every sparkling day.

The point is, at this juncture I don't want to get sidetracked into some pretend world. This body you gave me doesn't have a lot of mileage left on it; the calendar and the pharmacist have made that abundantly clear to me. Indeed, you and I wouldn't be talking like this today if it were not for the intervention of folks in long white lab coats whose chemical vocabulary is a foreign language to me. But thanks to you, there is another language we two know, and in that language of the heart, I have something big I need and want to say: "It's not comfortable standing down here at the river's edge, Lord. Sometimes I feel the water's chilly mist on my face. Always, always, I hear its constant flow. So, precious Lord, help me make the most of these Lazarus days. Guide my feet, hold my hand—help me do some good if I can, while I can."

---

* *The reference is to the biblical story of Lazarus, the friend of Jesus whom Jesus raised from the dead four days after his burial. See John 11.*

** *Helmut Thielicke,* Living with Death. *trans. Geoffrey W. Bromiley (Grand Rapids, MI: Eerdmans Publishing, 1983), 53.*

Scary

Why is dying so scary, Lord? Maybe others don't find it so, but I sure do. All our lives we laugh death off as though it is a joke. But if it is a joke, I'm finding it to be a very dirty one. I've been trying to identify where my fear comes from, and the best answers I've come up with are these two: the finality of death and my helplessness in its presence. Death means it's over. Death means there is no familiar tomorrow waiting. But all I have ever known is tomorrows! Eighty years of them! And now I'm told my supply is running out? That's incomprehensible! And terrifying.

Which leads to the helplessness of it. Though I may say, "I am dying," the deeper fact is that "I" am not doing one thing! The truth is that something is happening to me that I cannot stop. Forces are loose within me that are going to kill me regardless of how hard I fight or how much science my doctors throw at it. I am no longer in control of my dearest treasure—me.

For better or worse, I don't have much experience of being at another's disposal. And I certainly have none when my very existence is at stake. Despite all my professed faith, this is a scary time for me, God. Yes, I guess I ought to feel ashamed about this or apologize to you, but for the moment I'd rather just be honest with you about it. Maybe then you can calm my occasional times of sadness and steady my reluctant feet so I can walk toward the end (my unfamiliar tomorrow?) with hope.

Another Kind of Pain

Pain, as you know, had not been a part of my life prior to September 2021. Like the four-letter word that it is, pain had been unuttered and even unexperienced in my ever-so-fortunate life. But during that week in September, when the symptoms of this cancer began screaming at me, I self-diagnosed them as a brewing kidney stone attack. (And yes, descending kidney stones are gosh-awful as they plow their way down, but kidney stones do pass, as does their pain. But this . . . this wasn't passing!) Before I left the ER, where I first heard the diagnosis of prostate cancer, they began feeding me Gabapentin to combat my pain, and to my surprise they also slipped a vial of Percocet into my hand "for extreme pain." Thus, pills in hand, I was out on the streets in a tourist town in late-night darkness. Remembering it now, it was a perfect scene for how confused and frightened I felt. But the Gabapentin knocked off enough edges of pain that I slept well for the balance of that night in one of the few remaining motel rooms in the city. Fistfuls of Gabapentin continued to do the trick until I could get back home.

Then, while sitting in a radiation oncologist's exam room, I encountered yet another kind of pain. He was full of doctor-speak. Mary Carol and I had to drag plain English from him as though it were a second language for him. The upshot was that we were being told the cancer had spread so widely he didn't feel confident in the effectiveness of radiation in lessening my pain; my innards offered him so many targets that he wasn't sure where to aim his "bullets." He showed us the X-rays. My skeleton looked like a Dalmatian's hide, black spots everywhere. He shoved a booklet into our hands, turned to a certain chapter, and said, "Here's where you are." The chapter's title was "Stage Four."

Nobody had used that term before. As we left his exam room, he uttered a limp encouragement: "When the pain gets too bad, we can try some random treatments to see if we can ease it." (Someone else, trying to be helpful, told me cancer "can turn your bones into jelly.")

That night, in sleepless worry, I recalled the vial of Percocet. I got up from bed and went to the closet where it was stored. I shook it. Maybe half a dozen or so pills rattled back at me. That night, for the first time in my seventy-nine years, I thought of suicide. I understood why people kill themselves. *A half-dozen Percocet pills in one swallow. Now that ought to do it! I must hide these pills in a secure place; they may be my ticket out of here if my bones start to turn to jelly.*

For weeks upon weeks, Lord, the presence of that vial of Percocet was my secret exit plan.

What do you think about that, Lord? What would you have thought of me if, in hopeless pain, I'd chugged down a lethal dose of Percocet one night and ended it all?

House Money

I learned of a bright young woman, not yet fifty, who chose to have both breasts removed because a pathology report indicated cancer was present in one. As is usual, she then endured long weeks of chemotherapy and was clawing her way back to "normal" when her husband was diagnosed with a terminal illness. Within five years it had killed him—just as her cancer was reappearing. In months, cancer took her life.

And she was barely half my age! I absolutely cannot get my head around what must have gone through her mind in all that hell. Nor can I, in light of just this one case, justify my whining about this cancer of mine. As my friend Daryll said to me when he turned eighty, "Well, I feel like I've been playing with 'house money' for a decade already, so whatever happens from now is pure gravy!"* God, how I wish I had more of his spirit!

---

*"House money" is the money a gambler has won from the casino, or "house," so it costs him nothing to gamble with it. Psalm 90:10: "The days of our life are seventy years, or perhaps eighty, if we are strong . . . ."

Paying the Price of Love

A paragraph I saw today brought me up short. I started not to read it, since I could tell it was about grief and I'd always thought grief was a challenge survivors face. But since it was brief, I read it and was stopped in my tracks. In part, it said, "Grief is not a sign of weakness, nor a lack of faith . . . . It is the price of love." For the first time, I bumped up against the possibility that much of my emotional anguish wasn't just religious faithlessness or weakness; it was grief. You, God—more than anyone else—know how dismayed I had been that my faith was faulty and that I was such a crybaby. But the quote offered me another way to understand what was happening. In September 2021, my fantasy world of never dying was exposed; my invincibility bubble burst. That meant this life of mine, which has been such great fun to live, was on its way out. I have loved this life; I have loved this world. I have loved all of it so very, very much! Possibly too much. But now the party's over; it's time to go. No wonder I am often sad! I am paying the price of love. I am grieving!

I Hated that Monstrosity

As though it were burned into my brain is the sight of a folded black wheelchair. Without my knowledge, concerned friends quietly deposited it in our garage within days of the discovery of my cancer. Sincere thoughtfulness had prompted their action, but oh, God, I hated that monstrosity! I guess its donors had heard "stage 4" and something about "metastasis" and '"potent pain meds." They reasonably reckoned I would soon need a wheelchair, so they slipped one into the garage to be handy when needed. But every time I shuffled into the garage, every time I got into my car, that collapsible contraption stood there, wordlessly reminding me that further weakness and dependence were only a matter of time. That might be so, but I most certainly did not need nor did I want that metal sentinel silently mocking me every time I gutted out a smidgeon of mobility!

I am embarrassed that I could not see with a better spirit the caring that was present in that gift. Instead, all I saw was a hulking, unwanted intruder, biding its time until it could be an eager assistant on my inglorious descent into a cemetery pit. When I finally began to feel better, when the PSA numbers began to improve, I mustered the nerve to tell Mary Carol how much I wanted that thing GONE. Within a day it was. But to this day, almost every time I pass that corner of the garage I think of the wheelchair. Its empty space now looks sadly barren, crying out for something to fill its void. Once in a while, I dare to ask myself if that blank space represents me. Something very unwanted dominated me and filled my corner of the world for a while. Now it's absent. What is taking its place? I ask myself. Am I filling this miraculously open "space" with life? With the right kind of life?

Possible, Not Easy

I received a message from a lady who has suffered much. I loved her salutation: "Faith makes it possible, not easy." Perhaps these words are hers, wrung from her heartbreak.

Maybe they came from another's dark valley. Regardless of the author, these words speak a truth the bruised know best. "Faith makes it possible, not easy." Good stuff!

A Wild and Wonderful Meeting

When the worst of my bad news was fresh, I notified our twin sons. Though each lives a thousand miles away, they were both here within days. They came to be of support, to speak their love and prayers, to discern fitting ways to help. I insisted we also make a family trek to the bank and review the documents families usually review only after a death. Upon our arrival, our safe-deposit box was brought to us, and we retreated into a conference room and proceeded to have a phenomenally grand time.

As we worked through the Last Will and Testament and all the other fine print papers some families split up over, laughter filled the room. I wouldn't be surprised if the bank tellers wondered what we were drinking in there, but the only juice we shared was the wine of good memories. This or that bequeathal brought back memories of this or that event, and, as sure as lawyers love a "whereas" and codicils, after every lawyerly page someone at the table recalled something Aunt Lucille or Brother Pete had done or said, and we all chuckled and remembered an even better story about Mr. or Mrs. x, y, or z.

Even in the quiet moments of sharing information and clarifying picky details, a stunning tenderness reigned in that room. For all its solemnity, that was a surprisingly wild and wonderful meeting.

Upon returning the safe-deposit box to the wide-eyed, questioning bank employee, we headed to the lake with boxes of Mexican takeout and king-sized sodas to continue our odd party. At lake's edge and amid the nachos and the tortillas, my fifty-four-year-old boys got into a hilarious argument about which of them had first kissed Stacy, the high school dream girl of their youth—and would you believe it, to this day they're still carrying on this silly debate! Yes, we shed some crocodile tears of grief during that unplanned family reunion, but what I remember most is the silly laughter, the deep reservoir of memories, the hugs.

How can I thank you, God, for such a family? You know I did so little to be a notable father to those boys. Their mother "growed" them up while I was out trying to win the world to Jesus and (please, forgive me) also trying to become the world's Preacher Plenipotentiary. I failed both goals. Meantime, you and Mary Carol were back at the house, successfully developing some little boys into remarkable young men who delight me to this day. I don't deserve such. If those men truly need me for anything now, I don't know what it could be. But I thank you for the comforting notion that when my days end, two fine human beings bearing my name will fill my space so well. Whatever happens, I can't imagine ever being embarrassed to be called their daddy. Thank you.

Good Doctors

Not having been to medical school, I don't know what doctors are taught about relationships with patients. But, Lord, I hope you will place some extra stars in the crowns of two doctors who have treated me like royalty. When PSA testing showed prostate cancer had overtaken me, I sought the medical help of a urologist I knew through church channels. We weren't close friends, but he had sat through as many of my sermons as some of my deacons and hadn't bolted. I knew him; I respected him. And he's the one I cornered into telling me about the limited future I faced. He also told me there were some high-powered meds we could try once the already prescribed medication lessened in effectiveness. At the moment, that lifeline didn't feel too promising. All I heard was the twenty-four-month average. But the oddest thing that came from that conference (held on my back porch, no less—yes, an old-fashioned "house call"!) was our parting. It was as obvious as my tears that I was shaken by his candid news. I'm sure he'd seen that before, but as he left my home, he turned his full face toward me and, I suspect most atypically, reached out and hugged me, saying, "I'm sorry." That was an embrace I'm still feeling to this moment.

Weeks later I told him if I was going to die, I'd feel better about it if I had it confirmed by another doctor. He took no offense, giving me the impression he'd want the same if he were me. So it was that I arrived, an emotional wreck, in one of the exam rooms of a medical oncologist at Duke Cancer Institute.

Mary Carol and I were ushered in and put through the obligatory questions by the oncologist's assistant. Finishing her work, she smiled and left the room, saying the doctor would be with us soon. The following three minutes felt like four *Friday the 13th* movies, but then he quietly entered the room, introduced himself, and sat down with these words: "Well, your urologist has supplied me with all your records, and I have reviewed them. But why don't we begin with you telling me your story."

What? My story? You want to know my story? For the past three months I have been shuffled from one sterilized exam room to another, have been invaded as often as a dorm refrigerator, shoved into or put in front of a zillion machines, and for identification purposes have been asked my birthdate more often than I have celebrated it! But you, doc, you really want to know my story?

Lord, that very moment is when, for the first time in months, I began to feel hope—long before he said one word about any additional meds that might extend my life. His interest in my story was the first time I felt "humanized" since my urologist's hug. The intervening weeks had been a blur of clinical confirmations, necessary tests, and insurance-required procedures (thankfully, they were all done expertly), but the marathon left me feeling I was just one of an endless flow of bodies to be processed. But here was a doctor who wanted to hear my story! My story! What's more, he had a medication to prescribe that had a grand track record of thwarting the progress of prostate cancer.

God, I realize cancer can't be cured with hugs or humanizing, but surely such caring can't hurt. For myself, I know something broken within me began to feel whole again solely because that doctor thought I and my story mattered. I was so fortunate to have two "good" doctors, Lord. Please, let all who are hurting receive at least some of the same kind of help.

The One in Charge

When I awakened this morning, Lord, no one presented me with a menu of choices of how I wanted to feel today. That had already been determined elsewhere, without my consent. Obviously, my meds must be up and in full force because I'm feeling pretty good on this overcast morning, and I'm pleased by that. Three cheers for the pills!

The truth, however, is that I don't feel much like cheering about anything. I am no longer in control of much. And for a guy who has operated eighty years under the illusion that he was in control, I resent not being the one in charge! Okay, I admit that in a larger frame of reference, I have never been in charge of even a fraction of what I imagined was my turf. But Lord, I liked my false little world a whole lot more than I like this big unmanageable one. As I sit here talking to you, though, it's becoming clearer to me that one thing I do have a little control over is what I do with all this downtime. Maybe what I need to work on is figuring out how I want to spend this roller-coaster time of helplessness—and who I want to be during whatever time is still mine.

Every Soft Loop Whispered

I have apologized to the ladies, God. Now it's time to apologize to you. When my prognosis was the sorriest, a lady from the church I once served as pastor came to our front door bringing a shawl that was knitted and prayed over by ladies of the church. A week or so later, another lady delivered a second one, a "prayer shawl," they call it. I tried to accept both as graciously as I knew how, but on the backtrack of my mind I was battling so hard against an indicting memory that I am sure I flubbed my thank-yous. For I could remember when, during my tenure at the church, those ladies started this "silly" prayer shawl ministry. To my mind, shawls were associated with stooped and shuffling "widow-women," drafty old homes, and wooden walking sticks. But twenty years later, when two prayer shawls showed up in my lap, I was reduced to shame. Dadgummit!

Those women knew what they were doing all along! Soon thereafter came a chilly afternoon when, assured no one was watching, I embarrassedly slipped one of those shawls around my shoulders. The gentle embrace of that warm fabric was as close as I'll ever get to a hug from heaven. Every soft loop whispered concern and prayers for my well-being; every fiber radiated calming care. Very quickly, the eyes of a broken man filled with tears.

God, forgive my haughty stupidity in years gone by; and please tell me I wasn't that much of a jerk all the time. But also, God, thank you for women who knew and still know the human heart better than I do. Most of all, thank you for the comfort of being all wrapped up in someone's love and prayers.

The Rearview Mirror

Lord, it feels artificial to tell you about days and thoughts of my past as though you need the information or were ignorant and absent from all of it. We both know you were there back then just as you are here right now. You were my listening post then and you are my grand companion still. So please forgive me if I wander down memory lane as though you don't know these trails better than I did or ever will. But it is through memory that I often see your hand at work, and that is when I begin to realize how much I have to thank you for. I am also learning that it's through memory that I learn not to fret overly when I can't see your autograph on any current screen. I think I see you most clearly in the rearview mirror. It helps me not to panic in any seemingly God-forsaken present.

The backward glance strengthens my trust that you are still here and will be there in all that's waiting up ahead.

Being the Honoree

I have nothing to contribute to this conversation, Lord, except a question. How can folks like me know something yet not really know it at all? Specifically, all of us (theoretically) know we are dying. Still, we burn through our days as though the supply were infinite. Even though we know that everybody dies, we fail to include ourselves in that everybody. I have joked recently that I spent sixty years "doing" funerals, but only at age seventy-nine did I confront the fact that one day (soon) I would be the honoree. The very thought was shocking. More truthfully, I was offended, wounded. Why, God? Why have I found this diagnosis so outlandishly unexpected and unacceptable? What dwells within us that makes us deny and suppress the inevitability of our own death so ferociously? Or am I the only one? I don't think I am, if for no other reason than I cannot believe some would behave as they do if they had a lively awareness that "I, too, will die."

While the "Stuff" Percolated

I wish I were not so hung up about showy religion, Lord. I attribute it to Jesus's rebuke of the pious ones who tried to impress others with their religious garb and lofty prayers. (Of course, it could be that my disgust has more to do with my fear of being dubbed a fanatic.) This struggle was much in play the morning when the early testing was still underway—when they still insisted on pushing me around in a wheelchair.

They'd begun that morning by injecting some kind of radioactive "stuff" into my veins and then telling me to wait in the cavernous waiting area while the "stuff" percolated through my system. It would be a couple of hours before they could do the desired body scan, they said. Since I had been informed about the wait, I came well prepared with some good reading material. My Bible. That was a first for me. I take my Bible to church, not to the doctor's office. The latter falls into the category of showy religion. But that morning I was scared enough and sick enough that I didn't care what anyone thought. I needed something to hang on to! I needed a tangible connection to you. So it was that I sat in that mammoth waiting area for more than two hours, reading the first eight chapters of Romans until the technicians summoned me. I didn't bother to look up to see who passed while I was reading, nor did I care if they judged me as just another pitiful old man cramming for finals. I buried my head; I buried my heart in that book. I read. I read for my sanity; I read for hope. And I was rewarded. I found words of strength and a trickle of joy on those pages. I heard a quiet voice speaking across centuries into my quivering gut.

As frantic as I was, perhaps just clutching that book would have done the trick, although I doubt it. Even so, I hope those two hours will keep me from ever again thinking less of someone in a public place clutching a rosary or a Bible as though it were a talisman. I've been there. I've done that. And you helped me.

"And can any of you by worrying add a single hour to your span of life?"

—Jesus (Matthew 6:27, NRSV)

Waiting at the River

"The power of religion depends, in the last resort, upon the credibility of the banners it puts in the hands of men [sic] as they stand before death, or more accurately, as they walk, inevitably toward it."

—Peter Berger, *The Sacred Canopy: Elements of a Sociological Theory of Religion* (1967; reprint, New York: Anchor Books, 1990), 51

My Chosen "Myth"

Something has become clear to me through these past months, Lord. Belief in you is itself something of a miracle. To me it has been given to believe that you are and that you care. But there's certainly enough evidence out there for others to reach a very different conclusion! Some might dismiss my belief as the product of my believing parents and grandparents, but the fact is, I am now a believer. To put an even finer point on it, because of Jesus I believe you are a Jesus-like God. I'm not sure I'd be talking to you if it weren't for Jesus. My wager is that you are like him, and even if I am making a stupid human mistake by placing so much weight on this Christian turf, I think I will stand my ground. I find my chosen "myth" more satisfying than any alternative I know. For all the ways you have sneaked into my belief system, I give you thanks, O God. I'd be lost without you.

I Often Hear You

Many say prayer is a waste of time. I suppose there are some kinds of praying that are indeed a waste of time. But that's just my supposition. What I am sure of is my conviction that my conversations with you have never been a waste of time.

Critics of prayer say people like me are just talking to ourselves when we imagine we are talking to you. Maybe that's so, but I wish those detractors could account for all the benefit I've gained throughout my life from this habit of "just talking to myself." The way I see it, your expertise in listening and your restraint in replying is part of the grandness of prayer. Could I really reverence a God who jabbers as much as I do? That would be a big stretch for me. And as for your silence, I don't consider that to be evidence that nobody is listening so much as it is a reminder that you have done most of your speaking already—in the creation you fashioned, in the Son you gave, in the communion of those who call on you, in the holy texts that call me to use my brains as well as my heart to hear what you've already said. When I slow down to "hear" what a passing cloud or a budding flower are saying, when I'm among even a few folks who don't find prayer weird at all, when someone smiles at me or takes the time to listen to me ramble, when I open my Bible and "hear" a passage come alive with relevance, when I kneel to partake of your bread and cup—when any of that happens, I often hear you. And it motivates me to keep on talking. Thank you, God, for your ready ear, your big heart, and sufficient confidence in your works not to need a lot of talking.

Teach Me How to Let Go

Lord God, I keep running into biblical statements about losing one's life in order to gain it. Who in their right minds wants to think about losing their life? When Jesus told his disciples he was soon to die, they did not, could not, would not hear it. Nobody is ready to think about death; rather, we fight it! But if I am reading the Gospels correctly, the greatest gains in life—whether spiritual or physical—come when death is accepted. This goes against all I cherish, but I fear it is what I most need to ponder. By clutching today's life so dearly, am I forfeiting the birth of a richer Lazarus life today and the emergence of a healthy anticipation of the grander life awaiting me? Lord, I know how to clutch and hoard; teach me how to let go!

Precious?!

God, I've never found a satisfying interpretation of Psalm 116:15: "Precious in the sight of the Lord is the death of his faithful ones." Every way I've attempted to approach this sentence has been filled with potholes and ugly detours. But my pastor told a story this morning that gives me a fresh inroad.

She told of an obstetrician who was busily presiding over the birth of a newborn, being ever so precise about each detail to ensure a healthy outcome for mother and child. But at one moment in this delicate process, the doctor was cradling the infant in her hands when the newborn's eyes popped open, fastening on the doctor's face. The doctor realized her own face was the first thing this little child was seeing in this world, her new home. The physician melted in a new sense of wonder at the holiness of her daily work.

My mind, however, immediately thought of the "awaking" that Scripture sometimes uses to speak of our resurrection from the dead. I recalled my problem psalm and its declaration of your pleasure at our death. But might that verse be likened to the moment of a newborn's awaking from one world into a new one, and the "preciousness" of that moment be the vision of a kind and beautiful face waiting? I thought of your delight, God, of your joy as you cradle us into your eternity, and of your possible whisper: "Hello, little one! Welcome to my bigger wonder-world. I am so glad to see you, emerging from the great preparation. Come, enjoy all I have prepared!"

By whatever route we come, there arrives a moment when the old is left and the new begins. What a fascinating idea to picture that moment as one of great joy—within God's heart and ours. It is as the *Book of Common Prayer* hints: ". . . and though this body be destroyed, yet shall I see God; whom I shall see for myself and mine eyes shall behold, and not as a stranger."

Sustaining Hope

Lord God, what does it mean to hope? It is a humbling comedy to me that this cancer diagnosis came only days after the publisher sent me the freshly printed author's copy of my book about hope.* What is not so humorous is that I cannot recall being helped by that book's contents in the next months. I remain convinced that I wrote some good and true words within it. But the only truth advanced within it that marched with me into this cancer fray was and is my belief that you are good. You promised you would be, and I am clinging to your trustworthiness. Unlike many other cancer patients, I cannot say I have maintained a chipper attitude all the way or have ever been convinced I was going to beat this thing. None of that was true for me. I just did not know. The one and only thing I would dare say I knew is that I had a dogged belief that whether I lived or died, you would take care of me.

That, to me, was and still is my one grand hope. I could and cannot prove this, but in trusting it to be so, I am finding a sustaining hope. You, the God of hope, are my hope.

Lively Hope: A Taste of God's Tomorrow (Macon, GA: Nurturing Faith, 2021).

Having Invested So Much

One of the ancient Greek philosophers—I trust you know his name, although I've forgotten it—offered a pointed truth in his rumination about immortality. As I recall, the gist of his paragraphs was that if our death means the end of us—that there is no form of life after this one—then we will have no consciousness of our non-being, and therefore we ought not to concern ourselves about the matter. That's a clever and effective way to end the discussion, and I admit that in some moments I found relief from my anxiety in the philosopher's observation. But I cannot bring myself to imagine that having invested so much in me, in us, across so many years, you will simply shut the whole operation down, period. Blackout!

Perhaps I'm an incurable hoper, but I am determined to keep knocking on resurrection's door—as thick and impenetrable as it may be—because I am persuaded that just beyond our last breath here, you have something astonishingly breathtaking already waiting.

You Know

Lord God, it means so much to me that you know my heart and are not limited to my words as your only means of "reading" me. I take comfort in the declaration, "Even before a word is on my tongue, O Lord, you know it completely" (Psalm 139:4). I mention this because I worry that all you are hearing from me is my wonderings, my uneasiness, and yes, my fears. Yet you know that within me there also dwells an inexplicable trust in you. My soul rests on the bedrock belief that in life and in death you will not forget the work of your hands; you will not be deaf or blind to the path we walk, nor will your heart ever become uncaring. How can I sufficiently say thank you? "I am thine, O Lord." "I believe, Lord, help my unbelief."

Expecting Nothing in Return

Occasionally a flash of shame pierces through me, Lord. Is it sinfully selfish of me to anticipate an eternal life in heaven to follow this life? Are my notions about heaven just my craven hankerings painted in holy colors? Yes, I find enough within the Bible to substantiate my hope for everlasting life, but I still wonder sometimes if I—if all of us are reading into this more than we should. Maybe "everlasting" had significant overtones in the ancient world that are not the same as those that come to our minds. Maybe "everlasting" had to do only with a quality of life here and now rather than an extended quantity of life in a hereafter. Maybe longing for a heaven and all the rest that we preachers say is waiting is just our selfish craving for more. I wonder about this occasionally, God, and ask myself if I'd feel resentment if there were no heaven. Like a lot of other things down here by the river, God, this one makes me tremble. I don't want to "use" you, Lord. I want to love you, expecting nothing in return—but I know that's not likely and perhaps not even appropriate in light of the promises within your book. But, God of all things seen and unseen, help me so to live and die that even if there is no eternity with you, these earthly days of mine will bear witness to you, a God who held this pilgrim enthralled all my journey through.

Death as an Enabler of Life

There is a hint whispered often in the New Testament, Lord, and if my spirit could just hear and accept this hint half as clearly as it appears on the biblical page, all would be well. New life is possible, it says, but only after death to this life. I've wrestled with the concept of the necessity of death as an enabler of life ever since I began to hear it from Paul in Romans 6. Soon thereafter, I awakened to it within the sayings of Jesus: "Unless a grain of wheat falls into the earth and dies, it remains just a single grain; but if it dies, it bears much fruit" (John 12:24). In years past I heard this as a challenge to relinquish egotistical dreams and schemes, but I didn't warm to its counsel then any more than I do now. The difference is that now it seems to be calling me to let go of this biological life and assuring me of something better in return. What I once heard as a discipleship guide has now become a principle for living fruitfully and a secret for dying well. But dying is the door to both.

As I said, I've been wrestling with this for a long, long time, Lord. The best I know today is that I really do want to make my Lazarus days fruitful and my dying day victorious.

God, teach me how to rest in you so completely in this life that it won't be a farcical contortion when the promised life arrives.

Cards and Letters

They are within arm's reach of me right now, Lord. That packet of cards and letters I received in the fall of 2021 when the word went out about my illness. Every day our mailbox was stuffed with "get well" cards and handwritten notes from friends across decades and distances. At first Mary Carol brought them to me each day, and those anticipatory moments when I knew she was in the process of retrieving our mail and its certain stash of cards and notes for me were the emotional high point of my day. Going through them was like savoring the finest of gourmet meals, opening each envelope a solemn uncovering of today's sacred entrees. And I saved every one! There they are, carefully preserved in that packet, and someday I will again read my way through them with deep appreciation. Silly me, only now do I understand why Hallmark is such a huge company. I never knew how much even a paper expression of concern can mean when life has turned sour.

I, the Lord *your God, hold your hand;*
it is I who say to you, "Do not fear, I will help you."
—Isaiah 41:13 (NRSV)

Angels

One of the dismaying facets of the discovery of my cancer was remembering my mother's death from ovarian cancer in her eightieth year of life. Here we go again, I thought—like mother, like son! In so many ways I've always been just like Momma. She was the bookish one, the curious one, the fun one of my parents. At least in my mind, those have been my long suits, too. From earliest days I remember hearing, "Mildred, that little boy of yours looks exactly like you!" And we did resemble each other. Who am I kidding? Had my hair ever grown to Momma-length, they would have called me Danette rather than Danny. Too, mom couldn't utter a sentence without using her hands to interpret her meaning—nor have I ever been able to. And, of course, there is the weight issue. Bless her heart, Momma never saw a dessert she didn't want to sample, nor have I.

I respected my dad, but I really loved my mom, and watching her two-year chemo fight with cancer was gut-wrenching. I hated every day of it.

She died two dozen years ago, so I hadn't sharply felt her absence for quite a while. But when the doctors confirmed that I also might die of cancer at approximately the same age, Momma's story came roaring back to life. I was told (incorrectly, it turns out) that there is no relationship between her cancer and mine, but the correspondence was close enough that for the first time in my life I really wanted to tell her to get lost! She did not need to pass along all of her "stuff" to me!

My last visit with Momma was in her bedroom, and I noticed that the top of the chest of drawers at the foot of her bed was covered with little angel figurines. There must have been a dozen of them, but I recognized not one of them. This was not a display of familiar Mildred collectibles.

"What's up with the angels, Mom?" I asked.

"Oh, I have them there to keep me company."

"Really? Seems like with Dad and the aides and neighbors and church friends, you'd get tired of company."

"Sometimes I do. But a lot of the time I just watch my angels. There are some others who join them, you know. They come and go and smile at me—mostly at night."

I was speechless. Stunned. Was this her medications talking? That's surely possible, but I don't think so. Mom had always been devoutly religious, even teaching adult Sunday school classes for years. But she was no fanatic, not a weirdo, never prone to visions or wild ideas. She was a level-headed, Jesus-loving momma. But now here she was, telling me in matter-of-fact tones that she was living (and dying) in the company of angels!

Lord, I still don't know what to make of angels. Nor do I know what to make of Momma's report. But something inside me quietly hopes that when my own darkness deepens, I can once again be just like Momma—in the company of angels.

When Do I Get to Go Home?

Draped in gray, silent drizzle, the winter of '23 has arrived,
Autumn's banners of reds and golds now but a soggy carpet
And the breeze so recently soothing sends me hustling to the hearth.
With similar disruption, my spirit questions the descending season
With a bluntness the refined are taught to hide:
How many winters have I left?
Will this be the winter I get to go home,
Or need I layer up for a longer stay?
I ask you again, O winter, when do I get to go home?

    I suppose I'm ready now, or as ready as I will ever be for this trek,
    This long-joked-about, denied, avoided, and dreaded certainty.
    Odd how life, in blessing me greatly, has also done its number on me.
    Flesh that once was clear and smooth is speckled now with spots.
    Muscles that made it fun to run have cut and run
    Like yesterday's waistline, wit, and hair—fickle friends, all of them.
    So I'm ready now, I guess, as much as I will ever be, for the trek.
    Or will the weakness and grief of my public decomposing persist?
    Maybe this will be the winter I get to go home.

I speak of home as though I knew the place, although I've never seen it.
But then, I also speak to winter as though she were informed and chatty.

I once thought I knew a lot; now I question so much more.
I, the student with all the answers, have little now to say to me.
But though I be weaker, I hope I'm wiser for the run
Convinced it's not what I know but who I'm with
That will see me through.
For if a Jesus-like God deign to companion me,
His presence will be a happy home for my eternity.
I've been away for eighty-plus years.
Maybe the place is different now; I know I am.
Is this the winter I get to go home?

Your Stand-in

When the testing was complete and the facts ascertained, Ed called me. "May I come see you?" he asked. "Sure," I told him. "Midday is best, though."

The next day at eleven o'clock, he and I sat together on the back porch. Several years before I'd agreed to his request for me to speak at his funeral; now we clumsily agreed to swap places. I told him things I'd not yet had the guts to tell Mary Carol, mostly feelings. He asked for a copy of a hymn I'd discovered; its text was grand but its tune was unknown to me. I gave it to him, knowing he would have a good musician use it for my service. We stared at the floor silently, together, brothers in the ministry of Jesus Christ. He asked if he could pray with me. That's when I realized he was the first person who'd offered to pray with me since this started. He prayed while I listened and wept. We stood. We hugged. He left. But, God, I felt worlds better! He was your stand-in that day, Lord.

And a darned good one, too! In the weeks that followed others came by. One even left a cake on our front porch without ringing the doorbell—she didn't want to bother us, she later explained. All of them were your proxies, and I give you thanks for every one of them—and for all who prayed and cared from afar. How amazing is the power of friendship, Lord. In my Lazarus life, I want to make more such friends—and be one, too.

The Route

God, I was reading my Bible recently (I trust that meets with your approval!) and came upon Moses's recounting of the day when he and his rambunctious band of Hebrews came, for the first time, to the border of the promised land (Deut 1:22-33). The people wanted spies to go "explore the land . . . and bring back a report to us regarding the route by which we should go up." But when the spies returned and the Hebrews heard their report, they turned tail and ran, terrified by the news that "the people are stronger and taller than we and the cities are large and fortified up to heaven" (v. 28). So they spent an entire generation wandering around in the desolation of the Sinai Peninsula.

And you? Moses says you were miffed. You had promised to fight for and with them to occupy the promised land. Previously you had demolished the Egyptian power by leading the Hebrews out of slavery and then had carried them "just as one carries a child, all the way that you traveled until you came to this place" (v. 31). Throughout the entire journey, Lord, you had gone before them to "seek out a place for you to camp, in fire by night, and in the cloud by day, to show you the route you should take" (v. 33).

I chuckled when I read this final phrase about you showing them "the route" to take. That's the same word the people used to request some spies to go scout the land. We need someone to show us "the route," they said, as though they had previously been without a decent navigator! As though your leadership had been deficient. Your summation? "In spite of [all I've already done for you], you have no trust in the LORD your God, who goes before you on the way . . . ."

That's when I sensed this story is also about me. It's about my struggle to trust you with my fourth quarter. I have nothing but amazement and gratitude for all you've done to get me here, Lord, but I crave a clearer itinerary for the balance of my journey. I'd like to know how many more doctors and crises are in my future and if any more wheelchairs or assisted-living quarters await me before the end comes. I want to know the route! As awkward as it is to admit to you, the backward glance only goes so far in encouraging a trustful next step. Maybe that's what Fanny Crosby was admitting when she followed her stout hymnic declaration, "All the way my Savior leads me," with the sobering question, "Can I doubt his tender mercies who through life has been my guide?" The remaining stanzas of her song give me her answer. I am still working on mine. Day by day, choice by choice, mood by mood, I'm working on it, God.

Help me trust you to lead me "all the way."

All the way my Savior leads me; what have I to ask beside?
Can I doubt his tender mercies, who through life has been my guide?
Heavenly peace, divinest comfort, here by faith in him to dwell!
For I know whate'er befall me, Jesus doeth all things well;
for I know whate'er befall me, Jesus doeth all things well.
—Fanny Crosby (1820–1915)

A Fistful of Monopoly Money

It was a sobering moment, Lord, when I realized I have been serving you for my own sake. That revelation was humiliating. I'd thought I was being so noble, doing it all for you. But when the chips were down and you didn't come running to chase my boogerman away with a shout, I realized I'd been "believing" for decades on a contractual basis: if I do this for you, then you are obliged to do this for me. My self-concocted contract proved to be worth less than a fistful of Monopoly money. When I sensed this self-deceit lurking in my heart, I began to wonder if the same dynamic might be part of what the story of Jesus's raising of Lazarus is all about. Lazarus's sisters obviously thought Jesus should have come running when Lazarus got sick. But Jesus let his own friend die before he lifted one finger to help. So much for imagining you have a Miracle Man on retainer! My story is still ongoing, but I would like to learn how to live the balance of it without a contract—just trusting you to do what's best when the time is right. Yes, I still clutch a raggedy belief that in some way you do tend to those who love you. But I'm pretty sure it's silly to put a stopwatch on it or write a script on how you do it.

This World without Me

How vain I am, O God. I still recall with an embarrassed grin the day, early on, when I realized I could not imagine this world without me in it! How absurd that I could ever feel the whole world revolved around me, but truthfully, when I thought of this world without me at its center—observing, supervising, and griping—it was an impossible world to imagine! An hour spent in Atlanta's beehive airport could have shown me otherwise. "The world will little note, nor long remember" my presence here nor lament my absence. Yet, if Easter is true, there is some sense in which I will always be a part of your world. Right? All of this is so far above and beyond me, Lord.

Come, Holy One. Reduce my oversized ego and calm this spinning worrier; restore my soul to its rightful place.

Is This How Death Comes?

I had been taking the oncologist's miracle medication for less than a week when the next brick fell. I'd awakened that morning and taken a shower, feeling as weak as the proverbial cat and, as I toweled off, even a bit light in the head. Yet I finished dressing, wondering if the heavy sweater I pulled over my head might be too warm for what looked like a mild December morning. I remember I was perspiring lightly when I walked into the kitchen and sat on one of the kitchen barstools, trying to determine if my body was clammy from the shower's warm water or from the sweater. Mary Carol spoke cheerily to me, but as I attempted to answer, I could not! It was as though I were in a distant room, seeing her, hearing her, but unable to acknowledge her question about my breakfast desires. It was so odd!

She spoke again, and again I stared at her blankly, unable to respond. I did not slump or swoon or fall over but simply sat there like an inanimate object, mute. The next thing I remember is hearing her voice on the phone, summoning help, and then there was a buzz of people all about me, tearing off that sweater, lifting me onto a gurney, wheeling me out the front door. Not until we got halfway to the hospital did I begin to "come around" and find myself. A long day at the hospital revealed no answer for what had happened. They sent me home. They ordered a three-day Holter monitor to be strapped to my body. They said it showed I had an atrial fibrillation problem. They prescribed yet another dynamic medical duo: Eliquis and metoprolol. And thus it has been to this day. First, the blankety-blank cancer, and then, just in case I hadn't had enough, a "cardiac event."

As I now recall that kitchen episode, though, the thing that strikes me as most odd is that at no point in those befuddling moments did I ask myself, "Am I dying?" I did not wonder, "So is this the famous 'out of body' experience?" That didn't enter my mind! I knew something very strange was happening, but I was not filled with panic. I was not afraid. So now I ask, Lord, is this how death sometimes comes? Simply when we are aware that something odd is happening, and then our lights go out—or come on? Does death, when it comes, sneak up gently and do its work before we know it's happening? I wonder about this. God, I wonder about how it all goes down—or rises up.

A Descending Escalator

An airport I know has a train that conveys thousands of people from one terminal to another every hour. But this train runs on an underground track, and to board it you must take a descending escalator that appears to go down and down forever. Happily, from the top it looks well lighted down there, and on the parallel escalator you can see passengers by the hundreds coming up from the bowels of the earth. Still, I well remember my first encounter with this required descent into the invisible and my suspicious eyeing of the mechanical contrivance I was told to board. Yet I did so, and the first thing I knew I was safely in San Francisco!

Lord, in these months it sometimes feels like I'm eyeing that escalator once again. Only this time my destination isn't San Francisco, and I can dimly perceive the shadow of only one other traveler. Is it you? I'm still uneasy about this trip, but God, how grateful I am that even in this dark shaft, I can hear your voice and inexplicably feel your light leading the way. Is this my counterpart to "though I walk through the valley of the shadow of death, thou art with me" (Ps 23)? Whatever it is, I'm not yet a seasoned traveler, and the journey I'm taking is unfamiliar. "Guide my feet, hold my hand, lead me on, help me stand."

Let your gentleness be known to everyone. The Lord is near. Do not worry about anything, but in everything by prayer and supplication with thanksgiving let your requests be made known to God. And the peace of God, which surpasses all understanding, will guard your hearts and minds in Christ Jesus.

—Philippians 4:5-7 (NRSV)

You Brought Him Back to Life

Resurrection.

The word is as tantalizing as it is impenetrable. If resurrection means what I have learned to believe it means, Lord, then no human word is the final word. Even the word dead doesn't mean dead *dead* because you can resurrect the dead. My theology books insist that resurrection has nothing to do with the wonder of spring, when dormant roots and dry seeds spring to life. No, when I die, nothing dormant or dry will dawdle around to blossom next season; nor will something spiritual (my soul?) slip out and waft its way to the Better Place. No, the entirety of me will shut down. Kaput! But my books go on to say the good news of resurrection is that you, O God, are able to bring back to life what is genuinely, truly dead. My books tell me this is what you did with Jesus. He was stone-cold dead, yet you brought him back to life! His body was very different, but he was very much himself. And he was alive! This is the tantalizing aspect of resurrection: that you hold the keys to life and death and that you can bring us back to life as surely as you gave us life in the first place. What is impenetrable about this claim is the how of it, the when of it. I've yet to find a book that talks convincingly about this part of the mystery of resurrection. So, in mind-boggled perplexity, I drop all my bookishness and questions at your feet. Like a theatre patron confronting a suddenly pitch-black stage, I trust that the darkness is only for a change of scene, not the disappointing end of the show.

God, when these lungs you gave me exhale their last breath and this pulsating heart ceases to beat, I will be solely at your mercy. Sure, this dependence has always been true, but in that final moment it will be more keenly true than ever before. At that moment I will be only drying bones in a sack of flesh, a body awaiting "something." Lord, in your great mercy and holy time, raise me up to you.

"Am I Enough?"

I was sitting alone in the late-night darkness of my living room, Mary Carol having gone to bed an hour or so before. It was a quiet, sad time for me, O God. Yet it was also a sacred, good time too, a time to be alone with you. My mind wandered over a dozen chapters of my life, but always it then meandered back to the present and my life's apparent end. Each time I found myself returning to the terminal present, my spirit balked. All that had been was soon to be no more! "Nothing in my hands I bring" came to mind as I wrestled with the truth that there was nothing left now except you and me. It was one of the most solemn moments of my life. Nothing left but you and me! And, as clearly as if you yourself had spoken it, my mind whispered your humbling question to me: "Am I enough for you?"

I hope I will never forget that moment or how much honest soul-talk it took before I said, "Yes, you are enough."

Ill Prepared

I have one great, nagging regret about all the years I labored in your name as a pastor. I was so firmly denying my own mortality and thus so heedless of the weary quest for health being waged by those before me—especially the elderly—that I seldom if ever consciously crafted my words to speak to those who knew death was nearing their door. My denial, my flight from my own mortality, robbed them of the guidance you meant them to have. For this, I am truly sorry. And now, I myself have come to this hour ill prepared. For all the Sundays the dying sheep looked up and were not fed, dear God, forgive me. For all the confused moaning I now utter before you, evidence of homework undone, I ask your mercies.

What My Heart Was Feeling

I realize, Lord, that prayers are not to be rated like zucchinis at a county fair: Good, Better, and Best. However, I also realize that in my darkest days, one prayer was far and away the most difficult for me to pray. This was my Grand Prize Blue Ribbon winner. Its great difficulty rested in uttering it, in letting the words come up and out of my depths and into the audible world of real sound. I don't yet fully understand why it was so difficult for me to get this one simple sentence out of my mouth. Was it that I imagined I must, if I was a faithful minister of the gospel, respond to a diagnosis of a terminal illness with a submissive, non-protesting "Not my will but thine be done"? Was it that I knew you were aware of what was going on in my heart, and therefore it was pointless to blurt it out? Why was I so reticent, so long in finally groaning out these six one-syllable words? "God, I don't want to die!" Yet, as I let them flow out and into the air, my tears also overflowed, and a heavy load of something so unhealthy I still cannot name it exited. (Is this a slim sample of what exorcism is?) Whatever happened within those seconds of speech, it was liberating and rescuing finally to get my protest, my plea out into the air!

I don't for one minute believe my present Lazarus life is your answer to my protest—I've known too many others who have prayed similarly but nonetheless died. All I know is that I found a cleansing release of more "sickness" than I can name when I opened my mouth and let my entire body say what my heart was feeling. All I know is that I am still alive and miraculously able to do some things that bring me joy. The workings of prayer have always exceeded my powers of reason, Lord, but that "tough" prayer confirmed for me that John Bunyan was right: "the best prayers are groans." I thank you for that awful, wonderful day when I finally cried out, "God, I don't want to die!" Maybe you even smiled and thought, "Ah, now we're making some progress."

Her

Lord, I need to talk with you about Mary Carol. Yet as I do, I am relieved that you know what is in my heart more completely than my clunky words can express. (It's odd that I can talk more freely about my dying than I can talk about my love for my wife.) When we first married, though, I found it difficult to say "I love you" to her.

Those words seemed so high and also so very deep, even though that was what I truly felt. Now I find those words flowing from me as easily as "Hello." It is funny what living with someone for almost sixty years and raising two kids can do to your comfort zone! Not to mention all the fun and exciting times we've shared—and the lows we've endured, including this cancer diagnosis. Through all these solemn medical appointments, conferences, biopsies, injections, bleary-eyed mornings, and prolonged moodiness—through it all she has been a steady anchor. But now, after all these months of "full speed ahead," I think the stark probability of finishing her life as a widow is finally hitting her. How I wish I knew what to do to help her, Lord. But it's pretty clear that I can't even help myself very much.

The only idea I have is to be as honest with her as I can about what my body is saying, to share with her as much faith and hope as my soul can muster, and to hug her as often as I can. (But that's purely selfish, Lord; I need her hugs more than I need some of these pills I'm taking!) As prone as I am to be aware only of me, Lord, train my heart to pay attention to Mary Carol; she isn't enjoying this rodeo, either.

A Disgusted Druggie

For the last fifteen years, as I sat in my physician's exam rooms for annual check-ups, the assistants have stared at me disbelievingly when I told them I took no medications. But it was true! At least it was true until the fall of 2021. An aspirin tossed down two or three times a year for a headache captured my complete medication history. I have been one of the extremely fortunate, and I still am. But now I take a cluster of pills at breakfast and more with dinner, and these are just warm-ups for my bedtime treat of four horse pills I'm told need long hours and an empty stomach to do their best work.

I vividly recall where I was standing, and even the glass I was holding, on the first night I began trying to swallow those bedtime monsters. I knew they were my lifeline, so I had no choice but to gag until I finally began to get the hang of combining just so much water and tongue wiggling to slam them down. My resentment began weeks later. That's when I began to chafe with the realization of my utter dependence on these pills, pills that had to be taken at just the right time and in just the right amounts. More infuriating was that this necessity was to be the story of the balance of my life!

Since then, I have softened my resentment somewhat. Other folks' medication necessities make mine look like a walk in the park; and then there are those who are dying because they have no access to these miracle drugs or couldn't afford them if a pharmacy were next door. So I'm learning "to take my medicine"—the humbling as well as the pills. But, Lord, I question if I'll ever figure out how to balance my profound gratitude for these pills and my low-grade anger at having to fiddle with them at all! Surely, there are some essential spiritual lessons in all this, so I will try to keep my student ears open. Meantime, I'm still a disgusted druggie—but a grateful one, too.

You Are Present

I mean no disrespect to those who find icons helpful in their praying. But even after reading about it, I still don't understand iconography. Perhaps this is attributable to my very Protestant heritage. Pleasant scenes of nature may calm me and delight me with your creative beauty, God, but I don't use those landscapes to help me pray, and the only time I tried to talk with you while peering at a stylized image of Jesus, the conversation went nowhere. No, when I want to pray, I just start talking to you anywhere, in any posture, eyes open or closed. My assumption always is that you are present and that you are like Jesus—whom nobody has seen for quite a while, either.

I don't think I've ever thought of you as an old man with a white beard seated on an oversized throne with the whir of angel wings keeping you cool. And I don't see you as male or female or resembling anything human in form. I don't even think of you as having a form. You are just you. A holy presence. An attentive holy presence. YOU! The one who is there and here and everywhere. No doubt the faithful who use icons for their praying would say the same thing. But whoever taught me to trust that you are "closer than breathing and nearer than hands or feet," please give them a special blessing today. It's quite a miracle to face whatever happens with an inexplicable sense that you really are never far away and are more caring than this childish heart can imagine.

Friend or Enemy?

A well-meaning friend tells me death is our friend and that I ought to think of it that way. I politely tell my friend he has a twisted idea of friendship. I say this because Scripture calls death an enemy (1 Cor 15:26) and says it has a sting (15:55). Not to brag on you, Lord, but this is another time when the Bible feels nearer to the truth than my friend's drivel.

But once I get past my revulsion of this "death is a friend" nonsense, I realize something is being voiced here that I must think about. When a terribly mangled or broken being nears death, I am willing to say death can be a friend. But not when a child drowns or an innocent bystander is gunned down. "One size fits all" terminology gets us nowhere. But in my own case, my earthly friend is surely telling me something I need to hear. Resurrection faith opens an alternate way of framing death, a way that softens its "sting" by recasting death as an entrance into glories uncharted. If I think of death only as an enemy, I am left only with grief and loss and anger. But if I can also discipline myself to think of my approaching death as a door-opening friend, then gratitude and hope are given entrance into my sadness. Great God, even in death, you befriend me!

Judgment

Lately it has dawned on me, God, that we have never talked about judgment. I remember frightening sermons I heard as a boy warning me of an even more frightening judgment. All my theology books, at least the ones that talk about "last things," include something about judgment, but oddly I don't remember much from those sections! It's not something I worry about, and that's not because I am such a crown prince of virtue.

Somewhere along the way I became so persuaded of your all-including grace that I have effectively emptied my mind of the helplessness of an indicted me standing one day in your presence to be sentenced: "up" or "down." I could not be so confident, however, were it not for the judgment I believe you underwent on the cross for all of us. "He who did not withhold his own Son but gave him up for all of us, how will he not with him also give us everything else" (Rom 8:32)? For all my struggle with death, there is no adequate way to thank you that a fear of condemnation does not plague me. I have enough to fret about without adding divine judgment to my list.

"*I am the resurrection and the life. Those who believe in me, even though they die, will live....*"

—Jesus (John 11:25, NRSV)

Jesus Buckled

I read today that actor Sam Neill has been suffering from some form of deadly cancer for quite a while. In a recent interview, God, he acknowledged his diagnosis, being quick to add, "I'm not afraid of dying." I wondered if his prompt disclaimer was spoken as reassurance to his fans, a presumptuous declaration that his days of imminent danger are past: "I'm not afraid of dying anytime soon." But I don't think that's what he meant. I understood him to be denying that he has any fears as he faces his inevitable death. His statement alerted me to how often I have heard or read other celebrities bravely deny any fear of death and, contrariwise, how very few—if any—are quoted as admitting apprehension or even mild anxiety about their death. The majority view among the quotable seems to be that death is a nothing.

I am puzzled by this nonchalance, Lord. Especially since facing my own death has been anything but a picnic. Are these denials just an act, a Hollywood show of bravado to keep the audience happy? Or does Sam Neill have an inside track I've yet to discover? Is he a quietly pious man with such a super-strong, unparaded faith in you that to him death is just another bump on his certain road to heaven? If that is so, I am torn. On one hand, it would be wonderful to have a big dose of Sam's medicine soon. But on the other hand, I'm not sure I want to approach my death as being no big deal. It is a big deal to me!

It seems to me Jesus was "shaken" by the coming of his death. He talked about his soul being "troubled" (John 12:27) over what was about to happen; he "offered up loud cries and tears" to you as "the one who was able to save him from death" (Heb 5:7), and he fell on his face in prayer-sweat as the end neared.

Without minimizing the uniqueness and horror of his death, I think even Jesus's knees buckled when his death approached. Perhaps my observations about Jesus are self-justification for my struggles, Lord. But maybe not. Whatever they are, might you use or transform them into worthy paving stones to help me wobble home safely?

An Embarrassing Cartwheel

Lord, in the middle of worship last Sunday I was momentarily tempted to try a sincere but sure-to-be-embarrassing cartwheel down the center aisle. We were singing "Guide Me, O Thou Great Jehovah," a hymn by William Williams (1745) I have loved for years. But this was the first time I had truly heard the opening phrases of stanza 3: "When I tread the verge of Jordan, bid my anxious fears subside; death of death and hell's destruction, land me safe on Canaan's side." Whoa! Stop the pipe organ, folks! Did this hymn writer just confess having "anxious fears" about dying? My spirit shouted "Hallelujah!" and my body wanted to go acrobatic because here was someone, smack-dab in the big middle of Sunday morning worship, verifying my feelings. Here was a hymn writer confessing "anxious fears" about dying. Amazing! Fantastic!

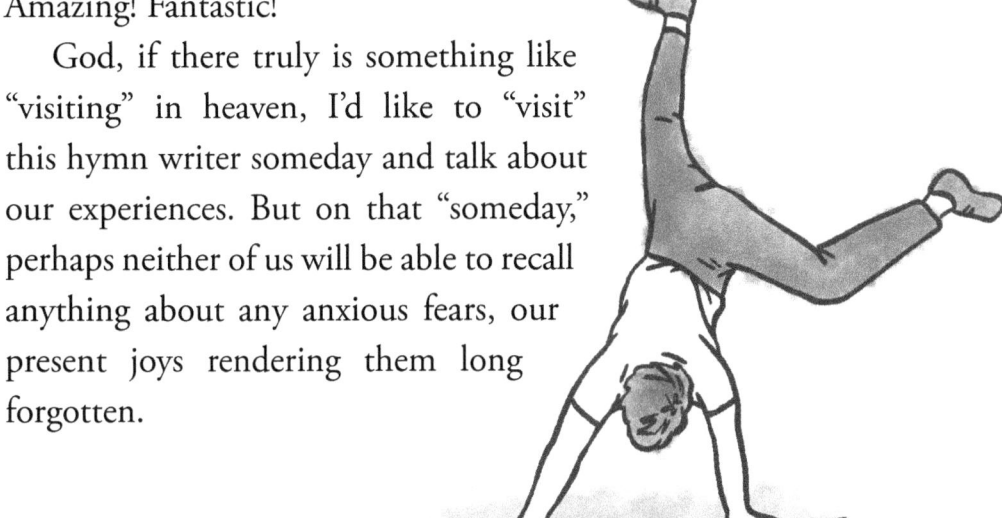

God, if there truly is something like "visiting" in heaven, I'd like to "visit" this hymn writer someday and talk about our experiences. But on that "someday," perhaps neither of us will be able to recall anything about any anxious fears, our present joys rendering them long forgotten.

His and Ours

Help me grasp something, Lord. I have little struggle affirming the resurrection of Jesus from the dead. That event is the anchor of my faith in you. But I am wrestling with the question of what his resurrection has to do with mine. In what way does Jesus's resurrection assure any of us a resurrection of our own? "Because I live, you shall live also" is a grand but somewhat unexplained promise—at least to my satisfaction. To date, the best I have come up with is the notion that Jesus is life, period. In him, there was and is life in its fullness. His invitation to me is to entrust my own life to him. To "give my heart to Jesus" is how I once would have said it. Today I'd probably say to lose myself in him and his way. But one of the consequences of that self-presentation is that even when this biological body of mine dies, all I've entrusted to him will not die because it's already become a part of the living one. I'm inseparably linked to the victor over death, to life. Being united with him in this life, I can be assured that this union will not be severed even in death.

Again, God, I realize that understanding the ins and outs of resurrection isn't required. But as long as this mind you gave me is intact, I want to use it on subjects deeper than the morning's cartoons. I know I am stepping off into the Great Mystery in this exploration, but I believe you are the one who had a little something to do with firing my curiosity in the first place.

Lazarus Life

Lord, I want to return to that "Lazarus life" idea we talked about earlier. It's a challenge that meets me most every morning. Since I'm no longer due in some office at a particular hour, my days are mostly mine to craft as I wish. I often question if the way I'm spending these days reflects my Lazarus-life status.

Some days I think my new life means I should be waiting tables in every soup kitchen in the county or handing out gospel tracts on street corners or marching in every protest parade or visiting every hurting soul I know. I've tried some of that and found the busyness of it both good and also lacking. So I then dive back into my natural habitat of contemplation and quietude, "drawing near to Thee." But that's not wholly satisfying either; there's only so much of the monkish path I can walk before it becomes a desert. How do I live as one who's been transferred from death to life?

Maybe I should live not so differently than before but with a deeper appreciation? I read that Marcel Proust once said, "The real voyage of discovery consists not in seeking new landscapes but in having new eyes." New eyes! I think new eyes may be your greatest gift to me through all of this, God. And one of my discoveries is seeing for the first time that life is not all about productivity. It is also good and God-pleasing to enjoy this world and all its wacky wonders. A jaunty flower, a good joke, a gorgeous sunrise, a symphony in full aural majesty, a phrase in holy Scripture, a plateful of my favorite foods, a hug from my wife, a lake at sunset, a thoughtful book, an old jacket that fits and smells just right, a story of faith and courage, a droplet of water as it forms and drips downward, a sky ablaze with stars, the melody of a beloved hymn, the spookiness of a dark, deep mountain canyon, the joy of my bed and its warm blankets when day is done. Great God! There is so much to enjoy!

I've been a lifelong child of duty—my teachers obviously drilled this into me quite successfully—to seek only one commendation: "Well done, thou good and faithful servant." Now I'm beginning to wonder if this wannabe faithful servant must also learn how to enjoy what you have made and lavished before me all my days. Maybe the only way this Lazarus will ever hear your "Well done" is if he can answer "Yes!" with a happy grin when you ask, "Well, Dan, did you enjoy my world? Isn't that Grand Canyon a hoot? And how about those Canadian Rockies or the ruby red I dreamed up for strawberries? Or camels with two humps? I'm rather fond of a baby's giggle myself."

Great and holy God, I want my Lazarus life to be filled with more times when I melt with joy and gratitude for the great privilege of just being your guest. I suspect you'd like that too.

P.S. Today I overheard someone quoting the famous line from the Westminster Shorter Catechism that solemnly declares, "the chief end of man is to glorify God and to enjoy him forever." Maybe, if I had been a Presbyterian, I would have seen this enjoyment angle earlier. But truthfully, the faithful Presbyterians I know appear to be grinding away just as much as I am.

An Adventure

Adventuring has never been my thing, Lord. Some of my friends thrive on hang-gliding, whitewater rafting, hiking the Appalachian Trail, and similar feats. My idea of an adventure is sitting down with a new book. But now the imperative of The Great Adventure confronts me. As I read Paul's death words, "the time of my departure has come" (2 Tim 4:6), I cannot ignore his overtones of great adventure. There's not a hint of dread or fear or even reluctance in him. He is "departing" for a better destination and seems eager for the journey to begin! I wish a similar allure would supplant the melancholy that grips me. I cannot speak disparagingly of those who seem so ready to depart and be with you. In fact, I envy them. I heard one guy speak of his life as being a series of away ballgames but now, finally, he's got a home game on the schedule. That's a bit simplistic for my taste, but I certainly get his point. My bookish bent is more attracted to the last reported words of Dietrich Bonhoeffer as he was taken from his prison cell to the gallows. To a friend he said, "This is the end; for me the beginning."* Lord God, I've got the first part of Bonhoeffer's words; help me find the peace and joy of the second. Help me taste the glory just around the curve.

---

* Dietrich Bonhoeffer, a young German theologian and a co-conspirator in the assassination plot against Hitler, was hanged on April 9, 1945, only days before the end of World War II.

Old Songs

That moment that follows our last breath--what happens to us then? Theologians have their cautious insights, Lord, but I prefer your book's artistry. In Revelation 7:18 I read that "the Lamb at the center of the throne will be their shepherd, and he will guide them to springs of the water of life, and God will wipe away every tear from their eyes." One of the attractive details of this beautiful scene is its declaration that the Lamb will be the one who ushers us to your heaven: "he will be their shepherd, and he will guide them to springs of the water of life." Somewhere, Lord, I picked up the notion that when the hour of death arrived, you would send the death angel to collect and carry us home. Did I get that from James Weldon Johnson?* But in this verse, I find a better word. Jesus himself does the collecting and the guiding! Wherever and whenever I die, he who died for me will be there. Jesus himself will take me home! I'm not sure why that means so much to me but it does, and maybe, like so many other matters of the heart, it goes back to my childhood.

When I was a lad, my mother's people spent holiday afternoons singing gospel songs around the upright piano in grandma's living room. One of those songs affirmed "I Won't Have to Cross Jordan Alone."** The song says, "When the darkness I see, He'll be waiting for me" and ends with a repetition of the reassuring promise, "I won't have to cross Jordan alone." During these past months, I have often recalled how much theology—good and bad—I picked up on those afternoons singing with "the old folks." Now, more than half a century later, it is remarkable how one of those old songs and a glowing phrase from Revelation wrap their arms around me to give an assurance that brings some peace. The Jesus I learned to love and trust when I was just a chubby little kid will be my companion all the way home. I won't have to cross Jordan alone!

James Weldon Johnson wrote God's Trombones *(New York: Viking Press, 1927), a collection of African American sermons as Johnson poetically reconceived them*

**Charles Durham and Thomas Ramsey, "I Won't Have to Cross Jordan Alone," Universal Publishing Group.*

A Mystery to Our Days

We went, Mary Carol and I, to St. Francis Springs Prayer Center to spend two nights in one of their hermitage cabins. One wall of our cabin's living room featured a floor to ceiling picture window. Easily visible across the way was an elevated cross, metal in composition, spare and black against the cloudless blue sky, and at its base there appeared to be some low stone walls. As the sun set, Mary Carol and I chose to explore our environs, and, as though magnetized, I headed first for that cross to investigate those stone walls. To my surprise, I discovered the entirety was a columbarium. A knee-high sign said, "Let us remember all our loved ones who are now celebrating their new life with the Lord." I wasn't prepared for that invitation or for this place, but hand in hand we made our way up the stone pathway to the base of the cross. We stood there for long moments in thick silence, shared a fierce, tender hug, and finally turned to walk away together, my every step heavy with the reckoning that soon she would be walking alone from such a place.

But here I now am, a full year later, and for the moment I am in enjoyable good health. The shock of those dreadful months of anxiety and that somber columbarium moment still roam inside me, but so does the wild upward ride that has followed. How can any of us mortals say what tomorrow holds? There is a mystery to our days, to our comings and our goings, that is known only to you, O God. There seems no rhyme nor reason to the number or quality of our days. Others, good and faithful souls, have sickened and died since I began this cancer journey. But since my days continue here, grant me so to live that at least a few might be glad my celebrating has been delayed. (Meantime, I myself celebrate the beauty and the quietness of places like St. Francis Springs, and I salute the Roman Catholics who built and maintain them—even for Protestants.)

Of Banners and the Heart

How do convictions grow into feelings?
    The question is not academic.
For my convictions wrap round a high banner proudly
    flying on my life's front yard
    while my clouded feelings, seeing no such banner,
    cower in the trench a stranger to my creed.
When mocking "facts" besiege my fickle heart, it folds.
    Sunday's soft "fear not" cringes, even crumbles, easy prey
    for Thursday's blaring, bully threat.

I've found no magic wand nor clergy trick to grow
    my mind's convictions into trust and steadfast laughter
So lacking better strategies I must
    train my heart to heed what I believe to be
    more than I tremble at what all can see
Before this growing season ends, by God,
    I mean to hold a harvest of quieted feelings
    and have a grateful hallelujah on this face,
    saluting my cherished shrouded banner—
and die with peace, a blind man seeing the invisible

My Capacity for the Beyond

Someday we must meet, you and I. Someday Mary Carol must awaken to a morning without me. Someday my sons must complete required forms, scribbling onto them the date Dad died. Someday these Jordan waters must be braved and I must cross to the other side. I do not know how or when, whether soon or late, but someday we will meet, you and I.

In some moments I feel it would be just fine if it were today. Yes, the imminence of the inevitable still seems an alien assault. Yet I have seen the dehumanizing effects of death too long delayed—of medicines holding at bay the release the body craves—and I dread the possibility of becoming another statistic in that column. Too, through all my adult years I have endorsed the glories of being at rest, at home with you. How disconcerting, then, that I still feel a queasy reluctance about the journey. The Apostle Paul (2 Tim 4:6f) seemed quite content with the nearness of his departure and receiving the heavenly prize; me, not so much. It is not that I fear having been self-deceived and discovering that hell is all there is for me. No, no! It is just that all of this is so threateningly different, so new to me. So beyond me.

I guess that is where I must leave it. With a prayer that you will help me in these winding down days to widen my capacity for the different, for the new, for the beyond—my capacity for you! Maybe, if our meeting day tarries for a while, I will learn not to be so distrustful of these waters but learn to welcome them and to find in their depths a path to beauty unimaginable, a path to you. Let it be, Lord. Let it be.

Deleted

I couldn't delete Bunky's phone number from my cell phone today. I bit my lip and let it be. He died last month. God, I'm not ready to let go of him (or me) yet.

A Trustworthy Witness

In the first weeks after learning the gravity of my condition, I turned to various prayer books hoping their words might help me utter my own—and, more truthfully, scouting for words others might use at my funeral. My favorite was waiting on page 504 of the Episcopal *Book of Common Prayer* in a section labeled "Additional Prayers." (Leave it to me to be attracted to something outside the stated liturgy!) One line leapt from the page: "when we shall have served you in our generation . . . may [we] be gathered to our ancestors." That line continues to resonate within me. My task, O God, has never been anything other than to be a trustworthy witness to you during the years given to me, to serve you in my generation. Yes, in my zealous youth, I hankered to make some big mark on the world so all generations would know of my stellar deeds. But somewhere along the way you helped me see my highest goal should be simply to write before the eyes of my contemporaries just another true sentence in your ancient, ongoing story. My sentence needs no gilded flourish; it needs only to further your story. And I, then, need to relinquish my pen to the coming generation and be gathered to my predecessors. The prayer book's words still say it all so very well. But to strengthen me, O Lord, allow me to pray the entire prayer, one more time:

> O God, whose days are without end,
> and whose mercies cannot be numbered:
> Make us, we pray, deeply aware of the shortness and uncertainty of
> human life;

and let your Holy Spirit lead us in holiness and righteousness all our
days;
that, when we shall have served you in our generation,
we may be gathered to our ancestors,
having the testimony of a good conscience,
in the communion of the Catholic Church,
in the confidence of a certain faith,
in the comfort of a religious and holy hope,
in favor with you, our God, and in perfect charity with the world.
All this we ask through Jesus Christ our Lord. Amen.

Another Quiet Night

It's another quiet night, Lord, and for once I'm not thinking about myself but about others who are wading through pensive days and long nights. Cecil, exhausted at the bedside of the once elegant lady who no longer knows his name or remembers the half century they shared as husband and wife. Marjorie, whose grown children ignored her birthday once again this week and contact her only when they need some information or cash. Ellen, who knows she's gay and also knows she will break her parents' hearts if she tells them. Jack and Barbara, whose brilliant son and only child will likely never see the outside of prison walls again. The widower across the street whose loneliness leaks unfiltered through his locked front door. All of us, God, are inching through our lives amid realities and feelings we despise. All of us, looking to you in our various ways, are dealing with death and dying and charged with living into and through it bravely. Lord God, hold us all in kind and merciful hands. Forgive us if our thoughts and actions are below our own standards, let alone yours. Help us to see every ray of sunshine and revel in their warmth; to receive with kindness every whisper of hope, every gesture of care; to trust that the best is still to come; and to walk on until . . . well, until your love is more tangible and our weariness is swallowed up within your glory.

A Winding Road

As June 2023 wore down, my oncologist told me my PSA number, rather than remaining in the basement, was creeping up the stairs. A royal disappointment! So now a new weapon is to be placed in my hand. More accurately, they are going to implant a catheter in my chest for a month and use it to take my blood from me, load up certain cells with cancer-fighting stuff, and then drip the doctored juice back into me. My assignment is to lie still on a fancy, inclined bed for hours on end while experts repeat this Dracula-magic three times across five weeks. The hope, of course, is that the third time will be the charm—or something like that.

Quite honestly, Lord, I am discouraged—devastated may be the better word—and apprehensive. I had hoped my assassin was more effectively stymied, that my days of freedom from concern would be greater in number. Plus, nobody can predict how well my body will respond to this new twist in my winding road. But I cannot kid myself: this road, like all roads, eventually leads to the river. So help me crawl up on that fancy bed of theirs and be a pleasant patient as the technicians go about their exacting tasks. They are doing their best to save my life, and I am grateful to them. But I am more grateful that you already have done that in ways too numerous to name. As I set my feet to this next unwanted path, O God, my prayer is that my steps, even if unsteady, will declare my faith more than my disappointment, my God more than my grief.

Solid Gold

Lord, I did not err when I told parishioners to cast all their cares upon you. Nor did I sell them snake oil when I urged them to trust in you with all their hearts. Those words were and remain solid gold. I regret only that I failed to add that this relinquishment is not easy to do. Life had not yet taught me how difficult it is to trust when the wheels are coming off. Now I am beginning to grasp why the Bible is so full of "trust in the Lord" admonitions. Could it be that nobody has *ever* found it easy to let go of the fear, the second-guessing, the discomfort of walking through life's shadowy valleys? Faith is so much harder than it looks. Certainly much harder than my sermons made it sound. Our senses are not trained to see the invisible, and our feet are not accustomed to walking in thick darkness. So, Great God, every time I gulp—swallowing down my dislike of today's path—help me also look up in gratitude and in readiness for all you have prepared, to all that is not yet seen by these little eyes of mine.

Just Beyond the River

Each one of these people of faith died not yet having in hand what was promised, but still believing. How did they do it? They . . . accepted the fact that they were transients in this world . . . they [were] looking for their true home. . . . they were after a far better country than that—heaven country. You can see why God is so proud of them, and has a City waiting for them.
(Heb 11: 13-16, The Message)

A Foreign Land

Years ago I ran across some scholar's declaration that "the past is like a foreign country; they do things differently back there." Ever since, I've tried to remember that wise observation when attempting to make sense of something from Sophocles or Deuteronomy or even the Gospel of John.

Historical research helps demystify some of it, but I still have often walked away suspecting I was missing so much because of my ignorance of that long-ago place and time. It now occurs to me that something of the same impenetrable mystery plagues me when I try to make sense of the future. It too is a foreign country, but for this one we have no reports, no research, and what I've read that presents itself as a *Fodor's* travel guide to eternity strikes me as well-intentioned ignorance parading as knowledge. Lord, your tomorrow is a foreign land! It's different! How I wish I knew more! So you who have drawn the curtains tight, help me handle this very visible here and now with as much kindness as I hope to receive in your invisible there and then.

The Soul's Eternal Home

Heaven. How I wish it were possible to rewrite the biblical descriptions! Pearly gates and golden streets? Really? I don't mean to be offensive, Lord, but these just don't do it for me! This sounds more like a chintzy amusement park than the soul's eternal home. An Atlantic beach scene at sunrise, a mountain range in snowy splendor, a Missouri meadow at sunset—you've done so many lovelier works than this gaudy city of John's imagination. I'm grateful for the scholars who have interpreted the features of the Revelation's vision of heaven symbolically and thereby rescued some of its more garish and unattractive aspects. But the whole scenario still doesn't work for me. John the revelator used the eyes of first century imagination and esthetics to "see" heaven. But to my twenty-first century eyes, what John describes doesn't get very far—I fear that if it's possible, I'll apply for a transfer (where?) asap.

So, Lord, I must trust that whatever heaven is, it will be better than the brochures John left for us and so much better than what any of us can begin to imagine. If, however, my complaints are disrespectful and my manner shameful, please forgive me and transform my sense of beauty and propriety as well as my body in your mysterious resurrection.

Forever and Ever and Ever

Eternity.

Like resurrection, it is a word that baffles me. When I was just a child, the word "eternity" terrified me. Something that goes on and on forever and ever and ever without end? That idea brought chill bumps to me whether we talked about heaven or hell. As much as I loved ice cream, even the prospect of having ice cream forever brought little excitement to me. I am no longer a child, Lord, and though years of education have expanded my ideas of eternity, the concept of a forever anything is eerily unsettling.

Eternal is a bit easier. I can think of it as something that is durable, dependable, trustworthy, a settled anchor in a rough storm. But eternity still evades me. My best help to date comes when I dismiss all my ideas of eternity as being endless time. I think of eternity as being the opposite of time. Eternity means time no longer exists. Eternity is a timeless existence—although I have no idea what a timeless existence might be like. Sometimes I think of eternity as being your time zone. If that is acceptable, then I find eternity less frightening. Eternity is to be with you. If you are anything close to being as fascinating as I believe, being with you would also be fascinating. Whatever may be the case, all of my ponderings here are surely only the childishness of a fretful old man. Yes, they are that, and more than that, they are my plea for you to visit me often, reminding me that I am not saved by how much I know but by your mercies.

A Fraction of the True World

I keep thinking about Momma and her visiting angels. Her words make me think of the Celtic concept of "thin places" where the invisible seems visible, where earth and heaven meet. These dual thoughts lead me to wonder if this world isn't always inhabited by more beings and more eternity than we in our busyness are prepared to see. Maybe this is part of what I mean when I speak of your nearness. Is it possible, Lord, that what we call the real world is only a fraction of the fuller, truer world of your creation? That death finally enables us to see all you have created instead of just our tiny part? To enter your whole world?

To Wander within Galaxies

My heart is more than ready
    for alluring images of your tomorrow
Those gates of pearl, those streets of gold
    filled with white-robed saints and holy angels hustling to
    rehearsals and smoke-filled vespers excite me not nor
    feed my starved imagination
So may I think of someday being freed to
    wander within galaxies of wonder
    set loose within the labyrinthine mystery of you
    timeless afternoons to ponder providence and joy shorn of
    disappointment, regret, and fear
    with sorrow's space filled by awe and laughter
Oh, yes! Great laughter will be a must
    to accompany the music your presence will mean
And if possible, might there be a wee-tiny horn
    for me to toot—just a note or two, now and then so
    none but you need hear my happy little Wow

Whatever Heaven Means

For privileged people like me, life can overflow with beauty and goodness and endless causes for gratitude. Some of us already have so much that the promise of heaven holds scant attraction. So when I think of heaven, I try to think not just of a heaven that answers the hopes of the rich but of a heaven that consoles the griefs of those whose life was hell. But God, my little brain and imagination just can't conceive of how you are going to satisfy us all. Perhaps that's one reason why I doubt heaven will be just a new and improved continuation of this creation. As stunning as the richness of this world is, I wonder if this was just your prototype, your trial creation, a hint of the perfect that is to come. Whatever heaven means, I suspect it will be so much more and other and lovelier than anything any of us have ever imagined. You who fashioned a universe filled with galaxies galore and trusted its care to tiny creatures like us, help us to do our duty now and prepare for splendor ahead.

The River?

Strange but longstanding is my dislike of water. As a boy I loathed my parents' Saturday night bath requirement, and to this day I remain baffled by others' obsession with showering daily. My settled conviction is that water is best for drinking, not for being in or on or flying over. And I have good reasons for this conviction.

As a ten-year-old, I reluctantly joined my Sunday school classmates for a party at Lake Okmulgee where our teacher had a motor boat and water skis. Never feeling safe around water, I clung to the inside of that boat the entire afternoon until all my excuses were used up. Against my better judgment I begrudgingly crawled overboard and slipped into the deep lake, my distrust of my flimsy life jacket doing absolutely nothing to diminish my fear of the water, which was already slapping me in the face. Sure enough, when the boat's motor roared into motion, it instantly jerked the rope that I'd been told would pull me up out of the water and propel me about, gliding on the water's surface. However, that rope only sucked me down into the water and dragged me around the lake for half an eternity, head first. I dared not let go of that silly rope—it truly was my lifeline!—but all my attempts to cry "Stop!" were rewarded only with another forced mouthful of lake water. It was not a good day.

Even the first baptism I ever performed, in the Red River, was not a good day. It was a muddy slog-hole mess. There was not one thing "holy" about that entire episode, except maybe the Holy Bible I carried with me out into the river, stupidly overlooking the fact that there was no dry shelf to place it on after I'd read (shouted) from it to the observing congregation.

So now here I am, a lifetime later, standing at "the river" without one pleasant association with such places. Of course, I know all of this "river" imagery is just imagery, a figure of speech and nothing else. But for me, Lord, it's an image that holds naught but fear and embarrassment. The longer I think about it, though, I don't remember there being anything mandatory about river imagery. When it came time for Moses to die, he just wandered off into the mountains and you buried him in some unknown valley in the land of Moab (Deuteronomy 34). This makes me wonder. I've always loved and felt the call of mountains, Lord. Given a choice, I'll choose the high country over a shoreline, any day, so is it all right, dear God, if I choose mountain imagery instead of river imagery? I can almost get homesick over the call of the high country. That feels right, that feels good. Especially when I note that you were the one who was up there on the heights with Moses, burying him in a valley within the mountains.

Making It

I was on the phone with Harold, and we were talking about Roland's recent death. Harold's summary: "The doctors did all they could and Roland fought like a gladiator, but he just didn't make it." How common that expression is, Lord, of death being due to someone's failure to "make it." I understand. To "make it" is to prevail, to survive, and if you don't "make it," the unsaid is that death beat you. That makes you a loser. On the other hand, I recall Millard Fuller's self-reported words when he discovered the lifeless body of Clarence Jordan out in his writing "shed" at Koinonia Farms. Viewing his fifty-six-year-old friend's body slumped against the wall, Fuller said, "You made it, Clarence! You made it!" Through his tears, Fuller's words were celebrating a victory, an enviable victory that his mentor and hero had just won.

It seems my task is to determine which of these outlooks will be mine: to view these Lazarus days as a descent into defeat or as a pilgrimage to a glowing horizon. Like it or not, as my pathologist friend once told me, "Dan, none of us is going to 'make it' out of here alive." His point is unarguable. But faith tells me more is going on in my dying than just the drumbeat of the inevitable. My faith tells me I can walk toward my "loss" with shoulders squared and spirit undaunted. My faith tells me that in this defeat there is also a victory, that in my growing weakness something is also being perfected.

I am personally persuaded that within all the mysterious majesty of Jesus's cry from the cross, "It is finished!" there is also a very human shout of victory. Whatever may have been accomplished for the world's sake that afternoon, this child of Mary and of Nazareth's byways knew he had run his life course faithfully. He'd made it to the end with integrity! A far horizon had been reached! Lord, I'd like to die like Jesus did, with a shout rather than a whimper. Help me keep my eyes on you and follow you—especially when this road gets rough or scary. Help me, Jesus. Help me make it.

Clarence Jordan (1912–1969) was a Georgia farmer with a PhD in New Testament Greek. He developed powerful insights into its relevance for a racist society that he offered the world through his Cotton Patch Version of the New Testament.

Doxology

If I had but one song to sing to you, O Lord, I would stand—if I could—and sing two hymns melded into one. After all my wonderings and my hopings and my frettings are done, these are my best, my truest, and my borrowed words:

Praise God, from whom all blessings flow; praise God all creatures here below.
Praise God above, ye heavenly host;
praise Father, Son, and Holy Ghost. (Thomas Ken, 1674)

For why? the Lord our God is good, God's mercy is for ever sure;
God's truth at all times firmly stood,
and shall from age to age endure. Amen. (William Kethe, 1561)

A Word to the Reader

Thank you for spending some of your minutes eavesdropping on my prayers. This likely means your life has also been turned upside down by the reality of death. My first impulse is to say that I am sorry, and indeed I am sorry any time the end of life must be faced. But I have also learned that there is great gain to be found in this encounter. Chief among them, for me, has been that I am no longer nearly as fearful of death as I was in the days when these conversations were first held.

Within my time of letting go, I have discovered an explosion of awareness of the everyday goodness and beauty surrounding me and have found a slowly emerging peace within. I hope both will persist. I pray you may know something of the same.

However, there is an unfairness in floating my story as a pattern because it is not. Many die so young as to make us feel cheated. Others of us die with a suddenness or rapidity that provides no time for preparation. And though today it appears I am being given a soft exit, who knows what tomorrow may hold? For all of us, regardless of the how or the when of our exit, the uniform fact is the Mystery awaiting us in that moment. I can only say that my trust in this Mystery as a Christly Friend rather than a Cosmic Stranger is more than precious to me.

Finally, a word of deepest thanks to my granddaughter Megan Grace Day for the illustrations and cover for this collection of conversations. All five of my grandchildren are "much above average," but I trust you can understand why I asked Megan to contribute to this effort. Every drawing arose from her creative mind and skillful hand in response to Granddad's words. Meg personifies the best of what I hope for the future, and to her and to the generations that follow, I look with joy and hope and thanksgiving.

Resources

In the quiet hours, when I sought guidance for my mind or spirit, each of these has repeatedly been a worthy helper.

Biblical Passages

Using various translations for my meditations has been helpful.
Isaiah 40–55
Psalm 23, 73
Romans 5–8
1 Corinthians 15
2 Corinthians 4–5
John 11
1 John 3
Revelation 21

Books

Long, Thomas G. *What Happens When We Die?* New York: Church Publishing, 2017.

MacNaughton, Wendy. *How to Say Goodbye: The Wisdom of Hospice Caregivers.* New York: Bloomsbury Publishing, 2023.

Nuland, Sherwin. *How We Die: Reflections on Life's Final Chapter.* New York: Vintage Books, 1993.

Perry, Gail, and Jill Perry, eds. *A Rumor of Angels: Quotations for Living, Dying, and Letting Go.* New York: Ballantine Books, 1998.

Thielicke, Helmut. *Living with Death*. Trans. Geoffrey W. Bromiley. Grand Rapids: Eerdmans, 1983.

Verhey, Alan. *The Christian Art of Dying: Learning from Jesus*. Grand Rapids: Eerdmans, 2011.

Wiman, Christian. *My Bright Abyss: Meditation of a Modern Believer*. New York: Farrar, Straus and Giroux, 2011.

Classical Music
Beethoven, *Piano Concerto No. 5 "Emperor," Adagio un poco mosso*
Beethoven, *Fifth Symphony*
Barber, *Adagio for Strings*
Massenet, *Meditation from Thais*
Dvorak, *9th Symphony, "New World," Largo*
Mussorgsky, *Pictures at an Exhibition*, "The Great Gate of Kiev"

Poetry
A world of luminous beauty awaits here. Pick your poet—and let the word-medicine work.

Conversations Alphabetized by Title

Preface, 1
The Door, 3

"Am I Enough?", 77
Adventure, An, 101
Angels, 59
Another Kind of Pain, 13
Another Quiet Night, 115
Being the Honoree, 33
Cards and Letters, 57
Death as an Enabler of Life, 55
Deleted, 111
Descending Escalator, A, 73
Disgusted Druggie, A, 85
Doxology, 139
Embarrassing Cartwheel, An, 95
Every Soft Loop Whispered, 29
Expecting Nothing in Return, 53
Fistful of Monopoly Money, A, 67
Foreign Land, A, 123
Forever and Ever and Ever, 127
Fraction of the True World, A, 129

Friend or Enemy?, 89
Good Doctors, 25
Having Invested So Much, 49
Her, 83
His and Ours, 97
House Money, 15
I Hated that Monstrosity, 19
I Often Hear You, 41
Ill Prepared, 79
Is This How Death Comes?, 71
Jesus Buckled, 93
Judgment, 91
Lazarus Life, 99
Making It, 137
My Capacity for the Beyond, 109
My Chosen "Myth", 39
Mystery to Our Days, A, 105
Of Banners and the Heart, 107
Old Songs, 103
One in Charge, The, 27
Possible, Not Easy, 21
Precious?!, 45
Rearview Mirror, The, 31
River?, The, 135
Route, The, 65
Scary, 11
Solid Gold, 119
Soul's Eternal Home, The, 125
Sustaining Hope, 47
Teach Me How to Let Go, 43
This World without Me, 69
To Wander within Galaxies, 131

Trustworthy Witness, A, 113
Twenty-four Months, 7
What My Heart Was Feeling, 81
Whatever Heaven Means, 133
When Do I Get to Go Home?, 61
While the "Stuff" Percolated, 35
Wild and Wonderful Meeting, A, 23
Winding Road, A, 117
You Are Present, 87
You Brought Him Back to Life, 75
You Know, 51
Your Stand-in, 63